AROUND TOWN

PUMPKIN PATCH

by Adeline J. Zimmerman

TABLE OF CONTENTS

WORDS TO KNOW

bumps

gourds

paints

pumpkin patch

round

stripes

PUMPKIN PATCH

Let's go to the pumpkin patch!

pumpkin

I see many pumpkins.

This one is big!

It is orange.

Gourds are small.

They are many colors.

This one has stripes.

This one has bumps.

I pick a round pumpkin.

He paints his!

LET'S REVIEW!

Point to the pumpkins. Point to the gourds. How do you know the difference?

INDEX